Guiney, Louise Imogen

England and yesterday

a book of short poems

Guiney, Louise Imogen

England and yesterday
a book of short poems

ISBN/EAN: 9783742895318

Manufactured in Europe, USA, Canada, Australia, Japa

Cover: Foto ©ninafisch / pixelio.de

Manufactured and distributed by brebook publishing software
(www.brebook.com)

Guiney, Louise Imogen

England and yesterday

CONTENTS.

PAGE

LONDON : SONNETS WRITTEN IN 1889.

    I.   On First Entering Westminster Abbey . . 3
    II.   Fog 4
    III.   Saint Peter-ad-Vincula 5
    IV.   Strikers in Hyde Park 6
    V.   Changes in the Temple 7
    VI.   The Lights of London 8
    VII.   Doves 9
    VIII.   In the Reading-Room of the British Museum 10
    IX.   Sunday Chimes in the City 11
    X.   A Porch in Belgravia 12
    XI.   York Stairs 13
    XII.   In the Docks 14

OXFORD : SONNETS WRITTEN THERE BETWEEN 1890
    AND 1895.

    I.   The Tow-Path 17
    II.   The Old Dial of Corpus 18
    III.   Ad Antiquarium 19
    IV.   Rooks in New College Gardens 20
    V.   On the Pre-Reformation Churches about
        Oxford 21
    VI.   On the Same (*continued*) 22
    VII.   A December Walk 23

OXFORD : SONNETS—*continued.*
  VIII. Undertones at Magdalen 24
    IX. Port Meadow 25
     X. Martyrs' Memorial 26
    XI. A Last View 27
   XII. Retrieval 28

LYRICS.
  A Ballad of Kenelm 31
  Two Irish Peasant Songs 33
  In a Ruin, after a Thunderstorm 35
  To a Child 36
  In a Perpendicular Church 37
  A Seventeenth-Century Song 37
  Columba and the Stork 38
  The Chantry 39
  April in Govilon 40
  On Leaving Winchester 41
  On the Cenotaph of the Prince Imperial in Saint
    George's Chapel 42
  Of Joan's Youth 43
  Passing the Minster 43
  The Yew-Tree 44
  Shropshire Landscape 45
  The Graham Tartan to a Graham 46
  In a London Street 46
  Athassel Abbey 47
  Romans in Dorset 49

LINES ON VARIOUS FLY-LEAVES.
  To Henry Howard, Earl of Surrey 53
  For Izaak Walton 53

PAGE

Lines on Various Fly-Leaves—*continued.*

A Footnote to a Famous Lyric 54
A Memory of a Breconshire Valley 56
Writ in my Lord Clarendon's "History of the
    Rebellion" 57
A Last Word on Shelley 57
An Epitaph for William Hazlitt 58
Emily Brontë 58
Pax Paganica 59
Valediction: R. L. S., 1894 59

vii

LONDON:
SONNETS WRITTEN IN 1889.

TO HERBERT E. CLARKE.

I.
ON FIRST ENTERING WESTMINSTER ABBEY.

Holy of England! since my light is short
And faint, O rather by the sun anew
Of timeless passion set my dial true,
That with thy saints and thee I may consort;
And wafted in the cool enshadowed port
Of poets, seem a little sail long due,
And be as one the call of memory drew
Unto the saddle void since Agincourt!
Not now for secular love's unquiet lease,
Receive my soul, who, rapt in thee erewhile,
Hath broken tryst with transitory things;
But seal with her a marriage and a peace
Eternal, on thine Edward's altar-isle,
Above the stormless sea of ended kings.

II.
FOG.

Like bodiless water passing in a sigh,
Through palsied streets the fatal shadows flow,
And in their sharp disastrous undertow
Suck in the morning sun, and all the sky.
The towery vista sinks upon the eye,
As if it heard the horns of Jericho,
Black and dissolved; nor could the founders know
How what was built so bright should daily die.
Thy mood with man's is broken and blent in,
City of Stains! and ache of thought doth drown
The generous light in which thy life began.
Great as thy dole is, smirchèd with his sin,
Greater and elder yet the love of man
Full in thy look, though the dark visor's down.

III.
S. PETER-AD-VINCULA.

Too well I know, pacing the place of awe,
Three queens, young save in trouble, moulder by;
More in his halo, Monmouth's mocking eye,
The eagle Essex in a harpy's claw;
Seymour and Dudley, and stout heads that saw
Sundown of Scotland: how with treasons lie
White martyrdoms; rank in a company
Breaker and builder of the eternal law.
Oft as I come, the bitter garden-row
Of ruined roses hanging from the stem,
Where winds of old defeat yet batter them,
Infects me: suddenly must I depart,
Ere thought of men's injustice then, and now,
Add to these aisles one other broken heart.

IV.
STRIKERS IN HYDE PARK.

A woof reversed the fatal shuttles weave,
How slow! but never once they slip the thread.
Hither, upon the Georgian idlers' tread,
Up spacious ways the lindens interleave,
Clouding the royal air since yester-eve,
Come men bereft of time, and scant of bread,
Loud, who were dumb, immortal, who were dead,
Through the cowed world their kingdom to retrieve.
What ails thee, England? Altar, mart, and grange
Dream of the knife by night; not so, not so,
The clear Republic waits the general throe,
Along her noonday mountains' open range.
God be with both! for one is young to know
Her mother's rote of evil and of change.

V.
CHANGES IN THE TEMPLE.

The cry is at thy gates, thou darling ground,
Again; for oft ere now thy children went
Beggared and wroth, and parting greeting sent
Some red old alley with a dial crowned;
Some house of honour, in a glory bound
With lives and deaths of spirits excellent;
Some tree, rude-taken from his kingly tent,
Hard by a little fountain's friendly sound.
O for Virginius' hand, if only that
Maintain the whole, and spoil these spoilings soon !
Better the scowling Strand should lose, alas,
Her walled oasis, and where once it was,
All mournful in the cleared quadrangle sat
Echo, and ivy, and the loitering moon.

VI.
THE LIGHTS OF LONDON.

The evenfall, so slow on hills, hath shot
Far down into the valley's cold extreme,
Untimely midnight; spire and roof and stream
Like fleeing spectres, shudder and are not.
The Hampstead hollies, from their sylvan plot
Yet cloudless, lean to watch, as in a dream,
From chaos climb, with many a hasty gleam,
London, one moment fallen and forgot.
Her booths begin to flare; her gases bright
Prick door and window; street and lane obscure
Sparkle and swarm with nothing true nor sure,
Full as a marsh of mist and winking light:
Heaven thickens over, heaven that cannot cure
Her tear by day, her fevered smile by night.

VII.
DOVES.

Ah, if man's boast and man's advance be vain !
And yonder bells of Bow, loud-echoing home,
And the lone Tree, foreknow it, and the Dome,
That monstrous island of the middle main ;
If each inheritor must sink again
Under his sires, as falleth where it clomb
Back on the gone wave the disheartened foam ?—
I crossed Cheapside, and this was in my brain.
What folly lies in forecasts and in fears !
Like a wide laughter sweet and opportune,
Wet from the fount, three hundred doves of Paul's
Shook their warm wings, drizzling the golden noon,
And in their rain-cloud vanished up the walls.
"God keeps," I said, "our little flock of years."

9

VIII.
IN THE READING-ROOM OF THE BRITISH MUSEUM.

Praised be the moon of books ! that doth above
A world of men, the sunken Past behold,
And colour spaces else too void and cold,
To make a very heaven again thereof;
As when the sun is set behind a grove,
And faintly unto nether ether rolled,
All night, his whiter image and his mould
Grows beautiful with looking on her love.
Thou, therefore, moon of so divine a ray,
Lend to our steps both fortitude and light !
Feebly along a venerable way
They climb the infinite, or perish quite ;
Nothing are days and deeds to such as they,
While in this liberal house thy face is bright.

IX.
SUNDAY CHIMES IN THE CITY.

Across the bridge, where in the morning blow
The wrinkled tide turns homeward, and is fain
Homeward to drag the black sea-goer's chain,
And the long yards by Dowgate dipping low ;
Across dispeopled ways, patient and slow,
Saint Magnus and Saint Dunstan call in vain :
From Wren's forgotten belfries, in the rain,
Down the blank wharves the dropping octaves go.
Forbid not these ! Though no man heed, they shower
A subtle beauty on the empty hour,
From all their dark throats aching and outblown ;
Aye in the prayerless places welcome most,
Like the last gull that up a naked coast
Deploys her white and steady wing, alone.

X.
A PORCH IN BELGRAVIA.

When, after dawn, the lordly houses hide
Till you fall foul of it, some piteous guest,
(Some girl the damp stones gather to their breast,
Her gold hair rough, her rebel garment wide,
Who sleeps, with all that luck and life denied
Camped round, and dreams how seaward and southwest
Blue over Devon farms the smoke-rings rest,
And sheep and lambs ascend the lit hillside,)
Dear, of your charity, speak low, step soft,
Pray for a sinner.   Planet-like and still,
Best hearts of all are sometimes set aloft
Only to see and pass, nor yet deplore
Even Wrong itself, crowned Wrong inscrutable,
Which cannot but have been, for evermore.

XI.
YORK STAIRS.

Many a musing eye returns to thee,
Against the formal street disconsolate,
Who kept in green domains thy bridal state,
With young tide-waters leaping at thy knee;
And lest the ravening smoke, and enmity
Corrode thee quite, thy lover sighs, and straight
Desires thee safe afar, too graceful gate!
Throned on a terrace of the Boboli.
Nay, nay, thy use is here.   Stand queenly thus
Till the next fury; teach the time and us
Leisure and will to draw a serious breath :
Not wholly where thou art the soul is cowed,
Nor the fooled capital proclaims aloud
Barter is god, while Beauty perisheth.

XII.
IN THE DOCKS.

Where the bales thunder till the day is done,
And the wild sounds with wilder odours cope;
Where over crouching sail and coiling rope,
Lascar and Moor along the gangway run;
Where stifled Thames spreads in the pallid sun,
A hive of anarchy from slope to slope;
Flag of my birth, my liberty, my hope,
I see thee at the masthead, joyous one!
O thou good guest! So oft as, young and warm,
To the home-wind thy hoisted colours bound,
Away, away from this too thoughtful ground,
Sodden with human trespass and despair,
Thee only, from the desert, from the storm,
A sick mind follows into Eden air.

14

OXFORD:
SONNETS WRITTEN THERE IN 1890 AND 1895.

TO LIONEL JOHNSON.

I.
THE TOW-PATH.

Furrow to furrow, oar to oar succeeds,
Each length away, more bright, more exquisite;
The sister shells that hither, thither flit,
Strew the long stream like dropping maple-seeds.
A comrade on the marge now lags, now leads,
Who with short calls his pace doth intermit:
An angry Pan, afoot; but if he sit,
Auspicious Pan among the river reeds.
West of the glowing hay-ricks, (tawny-black,
Where waters by their warm escarpments run),
Two lovers, slowly crossed from Kennington,
Print in the early dew a married track,
And drain the aroma'd eve, and spend the sun,
Ere, in laborious health, the crews come back.

II.
THE OLD DIAL OF CORPUS.

Warden of hours and ages, here I dwell,
Who saw young Keble pass, with sighing shook
For good unborn; and, towards a willow nook,
Pole, princely in the senate and the cell;
And doubting the near boom of Osney bell,
Turning on me that sweetly subtile look,
Erasmus, in his breast an Attic book:
Peacemakers all, their dreams to ashes fell.
Naught steadfast may I image nor attain
Save steadfast labour; futile must I grope
After my god, like him, inconstant bright.
But sun and shade must unto you remain
Alternately a symbol and a hope,
Men, spirits! of Emmanuel your Light.

III.
AD ANTIQUARIUM.
My gentle Aubrey, who in everything
Hadst of thy city's youth so lovely lust,
Yet never lineal to her towers august
Thy spirit could fix, or perfectly upbring,
Sleep, sleep! I ope, not unremembering,
Thy comely manuscript, and, interthrust,
Find delicate hueless leaves more sad than dust,
Two centuries unkissed of any spring.
Filling a homesick page beneath a lime,
Thy mood beheld, as mine thy debtor's now,
The endless terraces of ended Time,
Vague in green twilight.   Goodly was release
Into that Past where these poor leaves, and thou,
Do freshen in the air of eldest peace.

IV.
ROOKS IN NEW COLLEGE GARDENS.

Through rosy cloud, and over thorny towers,
Their wings with darkling autumn distance filled,
From Isis' valley border, hundred-hilled,
The rooks are crowding home as evening lowers:
Not for men only, and their musing hours,
By battled walls did gracious Wykeham build
These dewy spaces early sown and stilled,
These dearest inland melancholy bowers.
Blest birds! A book held open on the knee
Below, is all they guess of Adam's blight:
With surer art the while, and simpler rite,
They follow Truth in some monastic tree,
Where breathe against their docile breasts, by night,
The scholar's star, the star of sanctity.

V.
ON THE PRE-REFORMATION CHURCHES
ABOUT OXFORD.

Imperial Iffley, Cumnor bowered in green,
And Templar Sandford in the boatman's call,
And sweet-belled Appleton, and Marcham wall
That dost upon adoring ivies lean ;
Meek Binsey ; Dorchester, where streams convene
Bidding on graves thy solemn shadow fall;
Clear Cassington that soars perpetual ;
Holton and Hampton Poyle, and towers between :
If one of all in your sad courts that come,
Belovèd and disparted ! be your own,
Kin to the souls ye had, while yet endures
Some memory of a great communion known
At home in quarries of old Christendom,—
Ah, mark him : he will lay his cheek to yours.

VI.
ON THE SAME (CONTINUED).

Is this the end ?   Is this the pilgrim's day
For dread, for dereliction, and for tears ?
Rather, from grass and air and many spheres,
In prophecy his spirit sinks away ;
And under English eaves, more still than they,
Far-off, incoming, wonderful, he hears
The long-arrested, the believing years
Carry the sea-wall !   Shall he, sighing, say :
" Farewell to Faith, for she is dead at best
Who had such beauty " ? or, with kisses lain
For witness on her darkened doors, go by
With a new psalm : " O banished light so nigh !
Of them was I, who bore thee and who blest :
Even here remember me when thou shalt reign."

VII.
A DECEMBER WALK.

Whithersoever cold and fair ye flow,
Calm tides of moonlit midnight, bear my mind!
Past Christchurch gate, with leafy frost entwined,
And Merton in a huge tiara's glow,
And groves in bridal gossamers below
Saint Mary's armoured spire; and whence aligned
In altered eminence for dawn to find,
Sleep the droll Cæsars, hooded with the snow.
White sacraments of weather, shine on me!
Upbear my footfall, and my fancy sift,
Lest either blemish an ensainted ground
Spread so with childhood.   Bid with me, outbound,
On recollected wing mine angel drift
Across new spheres of immortality.

VIII.
UNDERTONES AT MAGDALEN.

Fair are the finer creature-sounds; of these
Is Magdalen full: her bees, the while they drop
Susurrant in the garth from weeds atop;
And round the priestless Pulpit, auguries
Of wrens in council from a hundred leas;
And Cherwell fish in laughter fain to stop
The water-plantain's way; and deer that crop
Delicious herbage under choral trees.
The cry for silver and gold in Christendom
Without, threads not her silence and her dark.
Only against the isolate Tower there break
Low rhythmic rumours of good men to come:
Invasive seas of hushed approach, that make
Memorial music, would the ear but hark.

IX.
PORT MEADOW.

The plain gives freedom.   Hither, from the town,
How oft a dreamer and a book of yore
Escaped the lamplit Square, and heard no more
From Cowley border surge the game's renown ;
But bade the vernal sky with spices drown
His head by Plato's in the grass, before
Yon oar that's never old, the sunset oar,
At Medley Lock was lain in music down !
So seeming far the confines and the crowd,
The gross routine, the cares that vex and tire,
From this large light, sad thoughts in it, high-driven,
Go happier than the inly-moving cloud
That lets her vesture fall, a floss of fire,
Abstracted, on the ivory hills of heaven.

X.
MARTYRS' MEMORIAL.

Such natural debts of love our Oxford knows,
So many ancient dues undesecrate,
I marvel how the landmark of a hate
For witness unto future time she chose;
How out of her corroborate ranks arose
The three, in great denial only great,
For Art's enshrining ! . . Thus, averted straight,
My soul to seek a holier captain goes :
That sweet adventurer whom Truth befell
Whenas the synagogues were watching not;
Whose crystal name on royal Oriel
Hangs like a shield; who to an outland spot
Led hence, beholds his Star; and counts it well
Of all his dear domain to live forgot.

XI.
A LAST VIEW.

Where down the glen, across the shallow ford,
Stretches the open aisle from scene to scene,
By halted horses silently we lean,
Gazing enchanted from our steeper sward.
How yon low loving skies of April hoard
An hundred pinnacles, and how with sheen
Of spike and ball her languid clouds between,
Grey Oxford grandly rises riverward !
Sweet on those dim long-dedicated walls,
Silver as rain the frugal sunshine falls ;
Slowly sad eyes resign them, bound afar.
Dear Beauty, dear Tradition, fare you well :
And powers that aye aglow in you, impel
Our quickening spirits from the slime we are.

XII.
RETRIEVAL.

Stars in the bosom of thy triple tide,
June air and ivy on thy gracile stone,
O glory of the West, as thou wert sown,
Be perfect: O miraculous, abide!
And still, for greatness flickering from thy side,
Eternal alchemist, upraise, enthrone
True heirs in true succession, later blown
From that same seed of fire which never died.
Nor love shall lack her solace, to behold
Ranged to the morrow's melancholy verge,
Thy lights uprisen in Thought's disclosing spaces;
And round some beacon-spirit, stable, old,
In radiant broad tumultuary surge
For ever, the young voices, the young faces.

LYRICS.

TO DORA SIGERSON SHORTER

AND

CLEMENT SHORTER.

A BALLAD OF KENELM.

"In Clent cow-batch, Kenelm, King born,
Lieth under a thorn."

It was a goodly child,
Sweet as the gusty May;
It was a knight that broke
On his play,
A fair and coaxing knight:
"O little liege!" said he,
"Thy sister bids thee come
After me.

"A pasture rolling west
Lies open to the sun,
Bright-shod with primroses
Doth it run;
And forty oaks be nigh,
Apart, and face to face,
And cow-bells all the morn
In the space.

"And there the sloethorn bush
Beside the water grows,
And hides her mocking head
Under snows;

31

Black stalks afoam with bloom,
And never a leaf hath she:
Thou crystal of the realm,
Follow me!"

Uplooked the undefiled:
"All things, ere I was born,
My sister found; now find
Me the thorn."
They travelled down the lane,
An hour's dust they made:
The belted breast of one
Bore a blade.

The primroses were out,
The aislèd oaks were green,
The cow-bells pleasantly
Tinked between;
The brook was beaded gold,
The thorn was burgeoning,
Where evil Ascobert
Slew the King.

He hid him in the ground,
Nor washed away the dyes,
Nor smoothed the fallen curls
From his eyes.
No father had the babe
To bless his bed forlorn;
No mother now to weep
By the thorn.

32

There fell upon that place
A shaft of heavenly light;
The thorn in Mercia spake
Ere the night:
" Beyond, a sister sees
Her crownèd period,
But at my root a lamb
Seeth God."

Unto each, even so.
As dew before the cloud,
The guilty glory passed
Of the proud.
Boy Kenelm has the song,
Saint Kenelm has the bower;
His thorn a thousand years
Is in flower!

TWO IRISH PEASANT SONGS.
I. IN LEINSTER.

I try to knead and spin, but my life is low the while.
Oh, I long to be alone, and walk abroad a mile,
Yet if I walk alone, and think of naught at all,
Why from me that's young should the wild tears fall?

The shower-stricken earth, the earth-coloured streams,
They breathe on me awake, and moan to me in dreams,
And yonder ivy fondling the broke castle-wall,
It pulls upon my heart till the wild tears fall.

D

The cabin-door looks down a furze-lighted hill,
And far as Leighlin Cross the fields are green and still;
But once I hear the blackbird in Leighlin hedges call,
The foolishness is on me, and the wild tears fall!

II. IN ULSTER.

'Tis the time o' the year, if the quicken-bough be
    staunch,
The green, like a breaker, rolls steady up the branch,
And surges in the spaces, and floods the trunk, and
    heaves
In jets of angry spray that is the under-white of leaves;
And from the thorn in companies the foamy petals fall,
And waves of jolly ivy wink along a windy wall.

'Tis the time o' the year the marsh is full of sound,
And good and glorious it is to smell the living ground.
The crimson-headed catkin shakes above the pasture-
    bars,
The daisy takes the middle field, and spangles it with
    stars,
And down the bank into the lane the primroses do crowd,
All coloured like the twilight moon, and spreading like
    a cloud !

'Tis the time o' the year, in early light and glad,
The lark has a music to drive a lover mad ;
The downs are dripping nightly, the breathèd damps
    arise,

34

Deliciously the freshets cool the grayling's golden eyes,
And lying in a row against the chilly north, the sheep
Inclose a place without a wind for little lambs to sleep.

'Tis the time o' the year I turn upon the height
To watch from my harrow the dance of going light;
And if before the sun be hid, come slowly up the vale
Honora with her dimpled throat, Honora with her pail,
Hey, but there's many a March for me, and many and
        many a lass!
I fall to work and song again, and let Honora pass.

IN A RUIN, AFTER A THUNDER-STORM.

Keep of the Norman, old to flood and cloud!
Thou dost reproach me with thy sunset look,
That in our common menace, I forsook
Hope, the last fear, and stood impartial proud:
Almost, almost, while ether spake aloud,
Death, from the smoking stones, my spirit shook
Into thy hollow as leaves into a brook, .
No more than they by heaven's assassins cowed.
But now thy thousand-scarrèd steep is flecked
With the calm kisses of the light delayed,
Breathe on me better valour: to subject
My soul to greed of life, and grow afraid
Lest, ere her fight's full term, the Architect
See downfall of the stronghold that He made.

TO A CHILD.

Dear Owain, when you are minded
To gather the perfect thing,
Over Abergavenny
Climb in the evening !—
I have seen where orchis dances
A saraband with the Spring ;

Where samphire leans to ocean,
And shakes in the word he saith ;
Or the brood of the peasant ragweed,
Innocent, sweet of breath,
Runs with a wild Welsh river
That never has heard of death ;

Where thrift, with a foot shell-tinted,
On the dark coast-road delays ;
And foxglove flames in a ruin ;
And campion meekly lays
On a crag's uneven shoulder
Her satiny cheek, for days.

Well : these in their mortal beauty,
And these in their youth, abound.
But over Abergavenny,
Past sunset-hour, I found
(O Holy Grail of a flower !)
The sun on the hilltop ground.

36

IN A PERPENDICULAR CHURCH.

The slackened arches never lose their beauty of alarm ;
The tall lines frown along the wall, like angels, sword
in arm ;
And where the vaults diverge, a grove with fancied snow
o'erspread,
Goes light among a myriad panes, with dust upon her
head.

England of old most innocent, whose flower of skill
achieved
Failed quick as Lammas lilies, when thy hand no more
believed,
What hast thou here, beloved but dead, held to thy
childless heart ?
Alas, thy human all of heaven : thine own and only Art.

A SEVENTEENTH-CENTURY SONG.

She alone of Shepherdesses
With her blue disdayning eyes,
Wo'd not hark a Kyng that dresses
All his lute in sighes :
Yet to winne
Katheryn,
I elect for mine Emprise.

None is like her, none above her,
Who so lifts my youth in me,
That a little more to love her

37

Were to leave her free !
But to winne
Katheryn,
Is mine utmost love's degree.

Distaunce, cold, delay, and danger,
Build the four walles of her bower ;
She's noe Sweete for any stranger,
She's noe valley flower :
And to winne
Katheryn,
To her height my heart can Tower !

Uppe to Beautie's promontory
I will climb, nor loudlie call
Perfect and escaping glory
Folly, if I fall :
Well to winne
Katheryn !
To be worth her is my all.

COLUMBA AND THE STORK.

The cliffs of Iona were red, with the moon to lee,
A finger of rock in the infinite wind and the sea ;
And white on the cliffs as a volley of spray down-flying,
The beautiful stork of Eiré indriven and dying.

I stole from the choir ; I fed him, I bathed his breast,
Till in late sunshine he lifted his wing to the west.

38

Oh, the bells of the Abbey were calling clearer and
        bolder,
And I feared the pale admonishing face at my shoulder.

Columb the saint's ! but I said, with mine arm in air,
(Of that banished body and homesick spirit aware,)
" The bird is of Eiré ; out of the storm I bore him ;
And lo, he is free, with the valleys of Eiré before him."

Of the man that was Eiré-born, and in exile yet,
This the reproach I had, and cannot forget,
This the reproach I had, and never another :
" Blessed art thou, to have lightened the heart of my
        brother ! "

THE CHANTRY.

A loyal lady young ; a knight for honour slain :
All beauty and all quiet sealed of old upon
Their images that lie in coif and morion.
A moment since, through rifts and pauses of the rain,
The day shot in ; the lancet window showered again
Its moth-like play of silver, rose, and sapphire ; shone
What arms of warring duchies glorious, bygone :
Lombardy, Desmond, Malta, suitored Aquitaine !
The while, aloft in Art's immortal summertide,
Fair is the carven hostel, fortunate either guest,
And men of moodier England pass, and hear outside
Fury of toil alone, and fate's diurnal storm,

Hearts with the King of Saints, hearts beating light and
      warm !
To these your courage give, that these attain your rest.

APRIL IN GOVILON.

Slowly, slowly darken
Primrose and pimpernel;
Heather of the rock, a-shake
On delicious air;
Slanted seas of spreading grass,
(Green glow and tidal swell,)
Under wind and pausing light how variably fair !

Larks from heaven descending
Hush; not a cloud-shadow,
Where so late the romping lambs
Chased it, in a ring;
High along a little wood
Quick rain-sparkles go;
Blorenge walls the faëry world: the sole substantial
      thing.

April in Govilon,
Filled with a bright heart-break;
Evenfall on dying wing,
Swanlike and supreme !
Soon, unheard, the Hyades
Run up the hills to take
Seven lamps, and trail the seven all night in Isca stream.

ON LEAVING WINCHESTER.

A palmer's kiss on thy familiar marge,
My oriel city, whence the soul hath sight
Of passional yesterdays, all gold and large,
Arising to enrich our narrow night:
Though others bless thee, who so blest before
Hath pastured, from the violent time apart,
And laved in supersensual light the heart
Alone with thy magnificent No More?

Sweet court of roses now, sweet camp of bees!
The hills that lean to thy white bed at dawn,
Hear, for the clash of raging dynasties,
Laughter of boys about a branchy lawn.
Hast thou a stain? Let ivy cover all;
Nor seem of greatness disinhabited,
While spirits in their wonted splendour tread
From close to close, by Wolvesey's idle wall.

Bright fins against thy lucid water leap,
And nigh thy towers the nesting wood-dove dwell;
Be lenient winter, and long moons, and sleep
Upon thee, but on me the sharp Farewell.
Happy art thou, O clad and crowned with rest!
Happy the shepherd (would that I were he!)
Whose early way is step for step with thee,
Whose old brow fades on thine immortal breast.

41

ON THE CENOTAPH OF THE PRINCE IMPERIAL IN SAINT GEORGE'S CHAPEL.

No young and exiled dust beneath is laid
In sole entail of high inheritance,
Though once compassion softly came, and made
A sleep at Windsor for the Son of France:
And sleep so long hath kept his image clear
Of pain's pollution, and the Zulu spear,
It seems his piteous self at last that lies
In prayer's old heart built to the island skies,
Low as the sifted snow is, and meek as Paradise.

Thus passeth all ye dream of might and grace !
Wherefore, beside the stones that cry it loud,
Let every musing spirit pause to trace
The cloud-burst of that Empire like a cloud;
And, looking on these stainless brows, proclaim
Peace unto Corsica's portentous name,
And peace to her, who in a sculptured boy,
Mould of her martyred beauty and her joy,
Reads here the end of Helen, the end of Helen's Troy.

OF JOAN'S YOUTH.

I would unto my fair restore
A simple thing:
The flushing cheek she had before!
Out-velveting
No more, no more,
By Severn shore,
The carmine grape, the moth's auroral wing.

Ah, say how winds in flooded grass
Unmoor the rose;
Or guileful ways the salmon pass
To sea, disclose;
For so, alas,
With Love, alas,
With fatal, fatal Love a girlhood goes.

PASSING THE MINSTER.

Praise to thine awful beauty, praise
And peace, O warden of my ways!
Bid o'er the brow to thee I raise,
Eternal unction fall.
Nobly and equally thou must
Take adoration of my dust,
And unto altitudes august
Thy low-born lover call.
Bless me; forget me not: a lone
Clear *Amen* through thine arches blown,
A heartstring of that Hope, a stone
Fixed also in that Wall.

THE YEW-TREE.

As I came homeward
At merry Christmas,
By the old church tower,
Through the churchyard grass,

And saw there, circled
With graves all about,
The yew-tree paternal,
The yew-tree devout,

Then this hot life-blood
Was hard to endure,
O Death! so I loved thee,
The sole love sure.

For stars slip in heaven,
They wander, they break:
But under the yew-tree
Not one heartache.

And ours, what failure
Renewed and avowed!
But ah, the long-buried
Is leal, and is proud.

Now I came homeward
At merry Christmas,
By the wise gray tower,
Through the green kind grass.

SHROPSHIRE LANDSCAPE.

Vague, in a silver sheen
Rayed from their armour green,
Some aged limes upstand ;
Nigh fields kindle and shine :
Beauty incarnadine !
What thrill of what Uranian wine
So flushed the placid land ?

All tints of a broken wave
Light the leafy architrave,
Far up the cloudy spring ;
And the ploughed soil ruddier glows
Than the ruby or the rose,
Or the moon, when the harvest goes
Beneath her blazing wing.

Trees keep the broad outpost ;
Dusk, by their dusky host,
Long-loved Severn glides.
Thence, towards the hilly south,
Like a queen, battle-wroth,
Upon a vermeil saddle-cloth,
The three-spired city rides.

THE GRAHAM TARTAN TO A GRAHAM.

Use me in honour : cherish me
As ivy from a sacred tree.
Mine in the winds of war to close
Around the armour of Montrose,
And kiss the death-wound of Dundee.

Yet fear not me, nor such estate
Heroic and inviolate ;
But green-and-white-and-azure wind
About thy body and thy mind,
And by that length enlarge thy fate !

IN A LONDON STREET.

Though sea and mount have beauty, and this but what
      it can,
Thrice fairer than their life the life here battling in the
      van,
The tragic gleam, the mist and grime,
The dread endearing stain of time,
The sullied heart of man.

Mine is the clotted sunshine, a bubble in the sky,
That where it dare not enter, steals in shrouded passion
      by ;
And mine the saffron river-sails,
And every plane-tree that avails
To rest an urban eye ;

46

The bells, the dripping gables, the tavern's corner glare
The cabs in firefly dartings, the barrel-organ's air,
Where one by one, or two by two,
The hatless babes are dancing through
The gutters of the square.

Not on Sicilian headlands of song and old desire,
My spirit chose her pleasure-house, but in the London
      mire :
Long, long alone she loves to pace,
And find a music in the place
As in a minster choir.

O deeds of awe and rapture ! O names of legendry !
Still is it most of joy within your altered pale to be,
Whose very ills I fain would slake,
Mine angels are, and help to make
In hell, a heaven for me.

ATHASSEL ABBEY.

Folly and Time have fashioned
Of thee a songless reed ;
O not-of-earth-impassioned !
Thy music's mute indeed.

Red from the chantry crannies
The orchids burn and swing,
And where the arch began is
Rest for a raven's wing ;

47

And up the dinted column
Quick tails of squirrels wave,
And black, prodigious, solemn,
A forest fills the nave.

Still faithfuller, still faster,
To ruin give thy heart:
Perfect before the Master
Aye as thou wert, thou art.

But I am wind that passes
In ignorance and tears,
Uplifted from the grasses,
Blown to the void of years,

Blown to the void, yet sighing
In thee to merge and cease,
Last breath of beauty's dying,
Of sanctity, of peace!

Though use nor place forever
Unto my soul befall,
By no belovèd river
Set in a saintly wall,

Do thou by builders given
Speech of the dumb to be,
Beneath thine open heaven,
Athassel! pray for me.

48

ROMANS IN DORSET. (TO A. B.)

A stupor on the heath,
And wrath along the sky;
Space everywhere; beneath,
The flat and treeless wold for us, with darkest noon on
      high.

Sullen quiet below,
But storm in upper air !
A wind from long ago,
In mouldy chambers of the cloud, had ripped an arras
      there,

And singed the triple gloom,
And let through, in a flame,
Crowned faces of old Rome:
Regnant, o'er Rome's abandoned ground, processional
      they came.

Uprisen like any sun,
Through vistas hollow gray,
Aloft, and one by one,
In brazen casque, the Emperors loomed large, and sank
      away.

In ovals of wan light,
Each warrior eye and mouth :
A pageant brutal bright,
As if, once over, loudly passed Jove's laughter in the
      south ;

And dimmer, these among,
Some cameo'd head aloof,
With ringlets heavy-hung,
As golden stone-crop comely grows around the castle
    roof.

An instant; gusts again,
Then heaven's impacted wall,
The hot insistent rain,
The thunder-shock : and of the Past, mirage no more
    at all.

No more the alien dream
Pursuing, as we went,
With glory's cursèd gleam ;
Nor sins of Cæsar's ruined line engulphed us, innocent.

The vision, great and dread,
Corroded ; sole in view
Was empty Egdon spread,
Her crimson summer weeds a-shake in tempest : but we
    knew

What Tacitus had borne
In that wrecked world we saw ;
And what, thine heart uptorn,
My Juvenal ! distraught with love of violated Law.

LINES ON VARIOUS FLY-LEAVES.

TO GWENLLIAN E. F. MORGAN.

.

TO HENRY HOWARD, EARL OF SURREY.

Young father-poet! much in you I praise
Adventure high, romantic, vehement,
All with inviolate honour sealed and blent,
To the axe-edge that cleft your soldier bays :
Your friendships too, your follies, whims, and frays ;
And, most, your verse, with strict imperious bent,
Heard sweetly as from some old harper's tent,
And surging in the listener's brain for days.
At Framlingham to-night, if there should be
No guest, beyond a sea-born wind that sighs,
No guard, save moonlight's crossed and trailing spears,
And I, your pilgrim, call you, O let me
In at the gate ! and smile into the eyes
That sought you, Surrey, down three hundred years.

FOR IZAAK WALTON.

Can trout allure the rod of yore
In Itchen stream to dip ?
Or lover of her banks restore
That sweet Socratic lip ?
Old fishing and wishing
Are over many a year.
O hush thee, O hush thee ! heart innocent and dear.

Again the foamy shallows fill,
The quiet clouds amass,
And soft as bees, by Catherine Hill
At dawn the anglers pass,

53

And follow the hollow,
In boughs to disappear.
O hush thee, O hush thee ! heart innocent and dear.

Nay, rise not now, nor with them take
One golden-freckled fool !
Thy sons to-day bring each an ache
For ancient arts to cool.
But, father, lie rather
Unhurt and idle near :
O hush thee, O hush thee ! heart innocent and dear.

While thought of thee to men is yet
A sylvan playfellow,
Ne'er by thy marble they forget
In pious cheer to go.
As air falls, the prayer falls
O'er kingly Winchester :
O hush thee, O hush thee ! heart innocent and dear.

A FOOT-NOTE TO A FAMOUS LYRIC.

True love's own talisman, which here
Shakespeare and Sidney failed to teach,
A steel-and-velvet Cavalier
Gave to our Saxon speech :

Chief miracle of theme and touch
That many envy and adore :
I could not love thee, dear, so much,
Loved I not Honour more.

No critic born since Charles was king,
But sighed in smiling, as he read :
" Here's theft of the supremest thing
A poet might have said ! "

Young knight and wit and beau, who won
Mid war's upheaval, ladies' praise,
Was't well of you, ere you had done,
To blight our modern bays ?

O yet to you, whose random hand
Struck from the dark whole gems like these,
(Archaic beauty, never planned
Nor reared by wan degrees,

Which leaves an artist poor, and Art
An earldom richer all her years ;)
To you, dead on your shield apart,
Be *Ave!* passed in tears.

'T was virtue's breath inflamed your lyre ;
Heroic from the heart it ran ;
Nor for the shedding of such fire
Lives, since, a manlier man.

And till your strophe sweet and bold
So lovely aye, so lonely long,
Love's self outdo, dear Lovelace ! hold
The parapets of song.

A MEMORY OF A BRECONSHIRE VALLEY.

—" *Patulis ubi vallibus errans,*
Subjacet aëriis montibus Isca pater."
Ad Posteros.

I.

I followed thee, wild stream of Paradise,
White Usk, forever showering the sunned bee
In the pink chestnut and the hawthorn tree;
And, all along, had magical surmise
Of mountains fluctuant in those vesper skies,
As unto mermen, caverned in mid-sea,
Far up the vast green reaches, soundlessly
The giant rollers form, and fall, and rise.
Above thy poet's dust, by yonder yew,
Ere distance perished, ere a star began,
His clear monastic measure, heard of few,
Through lonelier glens of mine own being ran;
And thou to me wert dear, because I knew
The God who made thee gracious, and the man.

II.

If, by that second lover's power controlled,
In sweet symbolic rite thy breath o'erfills
Fields of no war with vagrant daffodils,
From distance unto distance trailing gold;
If dazzling sands or thickets thee enfold,
Transfigured Usk, where from their mossy sills
Gray hamlets kiss thee, and by herded hills

Diviner run thy shallows than of old ;—
If intellectual these, O name thy Vaughan
Creator too : and close his memory keep,
Who from thy fountain, kind to him, hath drawn
Birth, energy, and joy ; devotion deep ;
A play of thought more mystic than the dawn ;
And death at home ; and centuried sylvan sleep.

WRIT IN MY LORD CLARENDON'S "HISTORY OF THE REBELLION."

How life hath cheapened, and how blank
The Worlde is ! like a fen
Where long ago unstainèd sank
The starrie gentlemen :
Since Marston Moor and Newbury drank
King Charles his gentlemen.

If Fate in any air accords
What Fate denied, O then
I ask to be among your Swordes,
My joyous gentlemen ;
Towards Honour's heaven to goe, and towards
King Charles his gentlemen !

A LAST WORD ON SHELLEY.

Each great inrolling wave, a league of sound,
All night, all day, the hostile crags confound
To merest snow and smoke.   The crags remain.

Smile at the storm for our safe poet's sake!
Not ever this ordainèd world shall break
That mounting, foolish, foam-bright heart again.

AN EPITAPH FOR WILLIAM HAZLITT.

Between the wet trees and the sorry steeple,
Keep, Time, in dark Soho, what once was Hazlitt,
Seeker of Truth, and finder oft of Beauty;

Beauty's a sinking light, ah, none too faithful;
But Truth, who leaves so here her spent pursuer,
Forgets not her great pawn: herself shall claim it.

Therefore sleep safe, thou dear and battling spirit,
Safe also on our earth, begetting ever
Some one love worth the ages and the nations!

Nothing falls under, to thine eyes eternal.
Sleep safe in dark Soho: the stars are shining;
Titian and Wordsworth live; the People marches.

EMILY BRONTË.

What sacramental hurt that brings
The terror of the truth of things,
Had changed thee?   Secret be it yet.
'T was thine, upon a headland set,
To view no isles of man's delight
With lyric foam in rainbow flight,
But all a-swing, a-gleam, mid slow uproar,
Black sea, and curved uncouth sea-bitten shore.

PAX PAGANICA.

Good oars, for Arnold's sake,
By Laleham lightly bound,
And near the bank, O soft,
Darling swan !
Let not the o'erweary wake
Anew from natal ground,
But where he slumbered oft,
Slumber on.

Be less than boat or bird,
The pensive stream along ;
No murmur make, nor gleam,
At his side.
Where was it he had heard
Of warfare and of wrong ?—
Not there, in any dream
Since he died.

VALEDICTION (R. L. S., 1894).

When from the vista of the Book I shrink,
From lauded pens that earn ignoble wage,
Begetting nothing joyous, nothing sage,
Nor keep with Shakespeare's use one golden link ;
When heavily my sanguine spirits sink,
To read too plain on each impostor page
Only of kings the broken lineage,
Well for my peace if then on thee I think,
Louis : our priest of letters, and our knight

With whose familiar baldric hope is girt,
From whose young hands she bears the Grail away.
All glad, all great! Truer because thou wert,
I am and must be; and in thy known light
Go down to dust, content with this my day.

www.ingramcontent.com/pod-product-compliance
Lightning Source LLC
Chambersburg PA
CBHW022027080426
42733CB00007B/761